DOUBLE-DIGIT RETURNS

DOUBLE-DIGIT RETURNS

IN GOOD MARKETS AND BAD

HARMEL S. RAYAT

Talia Jevan Properties, Inc.

100 – 9375 East Shea Blvd.
Scottsdale, AZ 85260

www.taliajevan.com

Although the author, Harmel S. Rayat, started his investment career in the stock brokerage industry, he is neither a registered investment advisor, broker, lawyer or tax expert, nor does he hold himself out to be one. This book is designed only to provide general information relating to the author's personal investment experiences solely for educational purposes, which means that the information is not intended as investment, legal or tax advice to any individual or as to any particular matter, whether it be business, investment, legal, procedural or otherwise. It reflects only the author's personal thoughts, opinions and experiences based on his personal investments over a period of several decades.

The results the author has achieved, as recounted in this book, were unique to him and you may not experience similar results even if you were to attempt to model your investment activities after the author's own. The author makes no representations or warranties that any investor will, or is likely to, achieve profits like those described in this book; past performance by one investor is not necessarily indicative of future results that another investor will achieve.

All investments, including real estate, are speculative in nature and involve substantial risk of loss of part or all your investment. The author strongly encourages you to invest carefully and to get personal advice from your professional investment, legal and accounting advisors as appropriate because the information provided in this book is not intended to replace or serve as a substitute for any legal, real estate, tax, or other professional advice; and, don't make any investment without first doing your homework (research and due diligence) and fully understanding the worst-case scenarios of that investment.

None of the material in this book takes into account individual investment objectives, financial situation or needs and is not intended as investment advice appropriate for any specific person. You must make your own independent decisions regarding any of the author's investment approaches described in this book.

References in this book to specific companies, in particular SolarWindow Technologies, Inc. and RenovaCare, Inc., are provided solely as examples reflecting the author's personal impact investment philosophy and are not

Cover designed by Monique McQueen

Library of Congress Cataloging-in-Publication Data has been applied for.

ISBN: 978-0-578-45322-4 (paperback)
ISBN: 978-0-578-46128-1 (ebook)
ISBN: 978-0-578-47286-7 (ePDF)
ISBN: 978-0-578-47287-4 (audiobook)

Printed in the United States of America

First paperback edition 2019

DOUBLE-DIGIT RETURNS

IN GOOD MARKETS AND BAD

RETURNS PER YEAR
SINCE 2006

7.5%	8.9%	9.4%	15%	45%
S&P 500	DOW JONES	FTSE NAREIT	NASDAQ	TALIA JEVAN

ANNUALIZED RETURNS FOR TALIA JEVAN PROPERTIES FOR THE 13 YEARS ENDED DECEMBER 31, 2018.

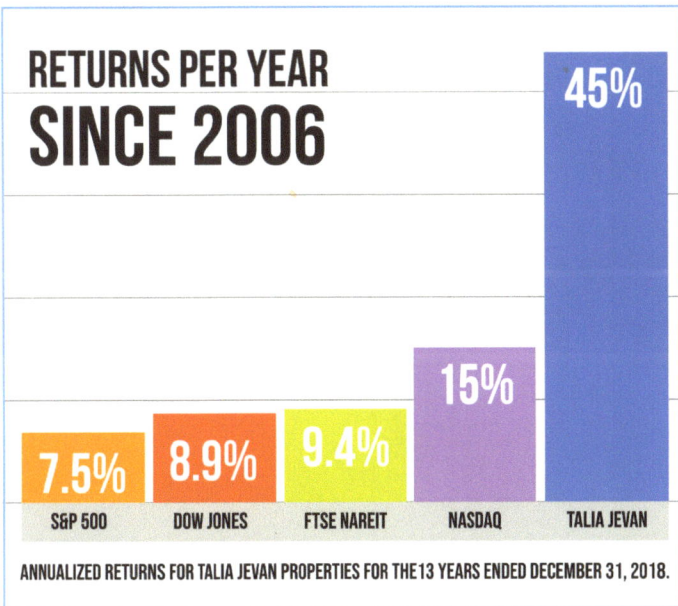

HARMEL S. RAYAT

CONTENTS

INTRODUCTION

There are two ways to learn; go for the easy way.

I am not a financial advisor, success coach or a motivational speaker, nor do I strive to be. In fact, the many great advisors and success coaches of today have forgotten more than I will ever know.

However, the one thing I do know is that life, in general, doesn't need to be so complicated. In some ways, life can actually be quite simple.

For example, you can learn through your own hard work or the intense effort of someone else. And, believe you me, it's much simpler and faster to learn from someone else.

You still have to work hard, but you'll have saved a lot of time not having to go through years of extensive training or gaining hands-on experience.

If you want to learn how to swim or play the piano, just find someone great at swimming or fantastic on the piano to teach you. If you want to make money, look around for someone that's already financially successful and learn from them.

I believe Tony Robbins calls this modeling, which involves finding someone achieving the results you want and mimicking their actions and thought processes.

To be candid, I wish I had mimicked more of the right people over the years. And, because I didn't, I have had my fair share of trials and tribulations, made plenty of mistakes, endured years of failure (more on this later) and, as a result, have more gray hair than I would like.

I often jokingly say that I went to the "School of Hard Knocks" and then attended the "University of Failure," graduating *summa cum laude*.

All kidding aside, I began my career working as a clerk and messenger boy in the mail room of a West Coast brokerage firm. Eventually, I got a job as a stockbroker. During my early years, I learned much from a few senior brokers, like Reg Ogden and Bill McWilliams, who held my hand and showed me the way.

After a while, I decided that I wanted to invest on my own, so I left the stock brokerage business in 1987, just months before the market crashed and the Dow dropped 23 percent in a single day. Although still the largest percentage drop ever, the market gyrations during 2018 felt just as big and just as scary.

Early on, many of my investments did poorly; some even failed outright. Luckily, the support of friends and family, alongside the inspiring mentorship of some seasoned investors and a few amazing people, pushed me to stay the course.

Thank goodness I took their advice and toughed it out. In hindsight, it's hard to imagine how I made it through all those challenging times.

Taking from the many hard lessons, I have since learned how to deploy capital in much better ways. Also, I have surrounded myself with a smart core team of executives who have been with me for years.

Today, I have a diversified portfolio ranging from institutional grade commercial real estate in the United States and Canada (discussed throughout this book) to significant equity interests in two innovative publicly-traded companies, SolarWindow Technologies and RenovaCare, discussed further in chapter 10.

Like every investor I know, my goal has always been to generate the highest risk-adjusted returns possible. However, market volatility, excessive fees, bad recommendations and conflicted advice always seem to get in the way.

So, wanting less risk, greater cash flow and some diversification, I decided to get into high-quality commercial real estate in 2006, forming the real estate arm of my family office (www.taliajevan.com). Almost immediately, my team and I started generating what many would characterize as exceptional returns.

Before I knew it, my portfolio was worth $50 million, with modest debt. Surprisingly, my returns got better and better. Unlike many, we sailed right through the so-called Great Recession; and, before too long, the value of my real estate portfolio zoomed right past the $100 million mark.

Since I started my career with little education and no money to speak of, it took quite a while for this reality to

The Birks Building was among the many buildings I visited as a mailroom clerk and messenger. Today, I am its proud owner.

set in. I still reminisce about my early days as a messenger, delivering packages in the pouring rain to many downtown buildings, including two that I proudly own today.

As mentioned, you can succeed through your own efforts or lessen the burden and learn from someone else's hard work. It's why cookbooks and recipes are so popular; all the heavy lifting has been done already—although you still must do the actual cooking.

I have intentionally written this book in a pithy, straighforward way to share the proven recipe that has worked so well for me in generating double-digit returns for so long, through good markets and bad. My mission is to share my hard-earned knowledge and strategies with all those interested, to help others as others have helped me; it's on of my ways of giving back.

When we started investing in real estate in 2006, we immediately broke away from conventionality and constrained thinking, placing the needs of others ahead of our own. My team and I treated everyone, not just our tenants, with respect, courtesy and integrity. "Honesty and unfailing integrity is good business," said Earl Nightingale. "Honesty is the best means of getting rich."

We relied on a factor more crucial than "location, location, location." Yes, there is something more important than location in real estate. You'll find out what it is in chapter 3.

We took on traits typical of luxury hoteliers, rather than typical of landlords. Shocking many, especially our tenants, we even lowered rents when we didn't have to.

After a decade in business, which included the tough years of 2008 and 2009, we retained leading appraisers to provide market valuations and engaged an independent accounting firm to perform an examination of our in-house investment returns in accordance with attestation standards set by the American Institute of Certified Public Accountants.

RETURNS PER YEAR
SINCE 2006

| | | | | 45% |

7.5%	8.9%	9.4%	15%	
S&P 500	DOW JONES	FTSE NAREIT	NASDAQ	TALIA JEVAN

ANNUALIZED RETURNS FOR TALIA JEVAN PROPERTIES FOR THE 13 YEARS ENDED DECEMBER 31, 2018.

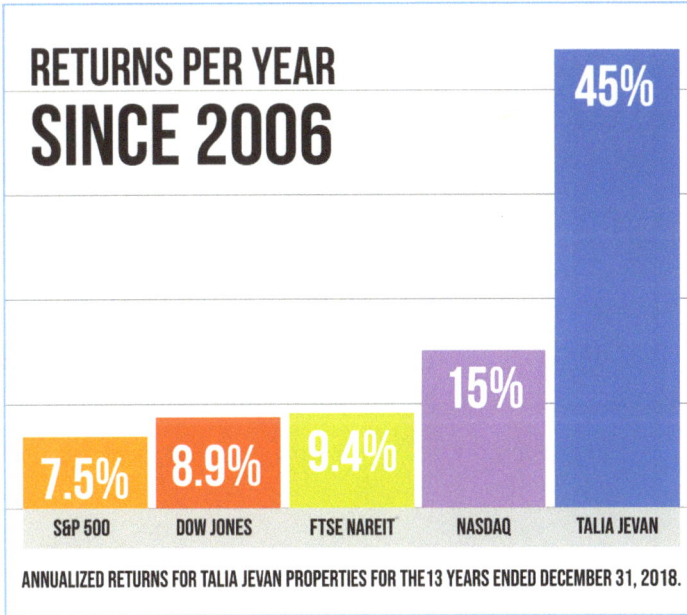

The Independent Accountant's Report that came back stopped me in my tracks: my team and I had generated annualized returns on equity of 33 percent per year (simple interest) for the 10 years ended December 31st, 2015.

In comparison, the S&P 500 had an annualized return of 6.4 percent, while the average hedge fund, as measured by the Credit Suisse All Hedge Fund Index, gained just 6.3 percent (in *total*, not per year), which works out to a scant 0.6 percent per year. Meanwhile, the FTSE Nareit All Index (an index of U.S. real estate investment trusts) gained about 95 percent, less than a third of the 326 percent in-house returns generated by my team and me.

More recently, for the 13 years ended December 31st, 2018, our relatively low-risk annualized returns stood at 45 percent per year, walloping most benchmarks and further validating the long-term financial benefits of the strategies revealed in this book.

During this same 13-year period, the NASDAQ generated annualized returns of 15 percent per year, while the Dow gained about 9 percent per year and the S&P 500 Index was up just 7.5 percent per year.

Of course, this is not to suggest that investing in publicly traded companies should be avoided. For investors and entrepreneurs with the right temperament, such investments can and do have the potential of generating significant returns, as early investors in Amazon, Facebook, Tesla and Netflix can surely attest.

In fact, I hold significant positions in public companies (described in chapter 10) which are chosen selectively and in alignment with my "impact" approach of investing.

As I said, I am not a financial advisor and the information in this book is not to be construed as financial advice or any other kind of recommendation; or, a solicitation of an offer to buy or sell any of the securities of any of the companies mentioned in the book.

Instead, I respectfully suggest the information in this book be viewed as a recipe, to be kept to yourself or shared freely amongst friends and family. Consequently, I have tried my very best to keep the concepts (or ingredients if you will) of this book easy to understand, simple to follow and quick to implement.

And, at any point, if you have any questions, need some clarification or want to share your thoughts and ideas, please reach out to me via LinkedIn, Twitter, Instagram, Facebook, or through my company's website (www.taliajevan.com).

Wishing you double-digit returns in the many years to come, in both good markets and bad.

1

MY START AS A MAILROOM CLERK

I still reminisce about my early days, delivering packages to buildings I own today.

My name is Harmel S. Rayat (www.harmelrayat.com). I'm no kid—I am in my late fifties with some gray hairs to prove it. My passions are helping people live better lives, music, technology, real estate and, of course, investing; I've been an investor for more than three decades.

I grew up in Vancouver, British Columbia. After graduating high school in 1979, I went to a local Vancouver community college for a program in small business and entrepreneurship, where Don Siemens mentored and guided me towards the brokerage business.

To get my foot in the door, I landed a job as a mail-room clerk and messenger boy for a large brokerage firm, Nesbitt Thomson Bongard. I would carry and deliver, by hand, pouches containing bonds, stock certificates and other important financial documents, worth, I assumed, a lot of money to a lot of people.

As part of my job, I often delivered items to the basement of a major bank through a building now renamed as the Birks Building, an iconic downtown Vancouver landmark, which, 26 years later, I acquired and still own (see photo on page v of the Introduction).

It was a menial job to be sure, but I was exposed to and able to talk with many smart stockbrokers. Some of what I learned at the time just came from watching and listening. Even more came from asking questions of, and getting answers and a bit of advice from, the successful brokers I came in contact with. Yes, I was, as Tony Robbins would say, "modeling" even back then in order to incorporate what I learned into my efforts to become a stockbroker.

I tried my very best to land a job as a broker myself but was turned down by just about every investment firm, from the bucket shops to the white shoe firms of the day. At the time, I was told I was too young, had little education to speak of and had no moneyed connections.

After being turned down by just about every firm, in 1982 I finally moved up from being a mailroom clerk to a full-fledged stockbroker.

Although deflated, I was not going to let someone else dictate my future. Finally, in 1982, I moved up from being a clerk and a messenger to being a full-fledged stockbroker at Canarim Investment Corporation (now Canaccord Genuity Group Inc.), again thanks to Don Siemens, who somehow was able to open the one door that led directly to the palatial private office of the then president of the firm, Peter Brown. It was a relatively short interview, and I am not exactly sure what I said or did to land the job, but I did. I will forever be grateful because his decision to hire me changed my life.

3

As part of my on-the-job training, I spent time on the trading desk of Canarim and on the trading floor of the now-closed Vancouver Stock Exchange, which today has been repurposed into a hotel and office tower to accommodate the continued population growth of Vancouver. Soon, I was assigned my own desk and given the Yellow Pages to start prospecting and cold calling for customers, which was very tough work. To this day, I try my best to take "cold calls" from individuals looking to build their business. At the end of each call, I wish them luck and encourage them to keep making those dials.

After many, many such calls, I made some headway and slowly started to reel in customers. To commemorate my very first order on August 4th, 1982, I kept the now faded, but originally blue-colored trading ticket, time-stamped at 9:50 am. It's framed now and hanging in my office, which is in a building I used to deliver to as a messenger and now proudly own.

Although I worked hard at it for a number of years, the brokerage business was not for me. You see, to make a good living, you have to recommend new stocks to your clients constantly. Are there really that many good stock bargains around at any one time? If so, why did the world's greatest stock investor, Warren Buffett, a man I also like to emulate, say that he finds only two great ideas a year?

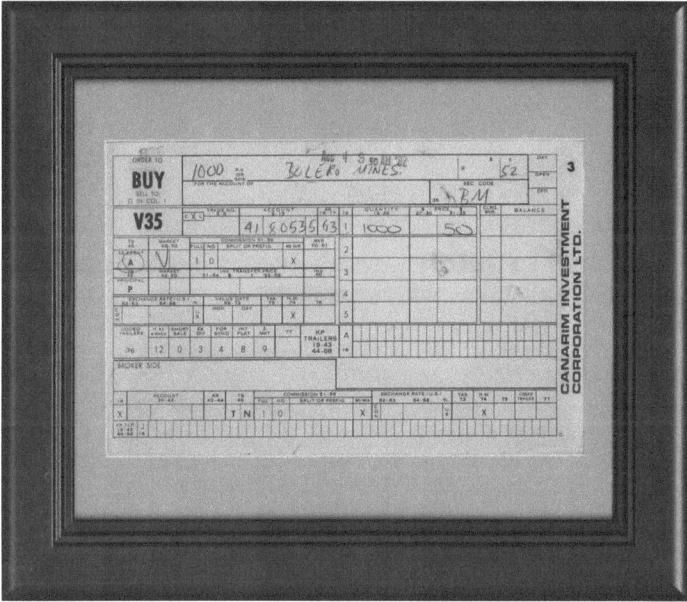

To commemorate my very first trade as a stockbroker in 1982, I kept the trading ticket which is now framed and hanging in my office.

So, in 1987, just before the stock market crash, I left the brokerage business and started investing on my own, in earnest, in companies with great products. I also tried my hand at starting and managing a few small businesses, ranging from old tech auto salvage to a few new-tech technology companies. However, not every business I invested in or started did well; some failed outright, including my auto dismantling business.

Between the loss of my mother and business failures, I hit a low point in my life. No matter how bright and sunny the days were, all I saw were dark clouds. With the passage of time and a lot of help and support from my family and friends, my lugubrious state of mind slowly but surely cleared.

Many pounds lighter from my depressed state, I went back to work and eventually regained my stride. I have always loved science and technology, so I decided to become a venture capitalist. I would back companies with promising technologies, fund them with some of my own money and raise the rest mainly through friends, family and stock offerings to outside investors. This is an age-old strategy used by everyone from first-time real estate investors and cash-strapped entrepreneurs to even the founder of one of the greatest tech companies of all time, Jeff Bezos (see chapter 9).

Although a potential return and profit is a factor in my investment decisions, my primary motivator has been, and continues to be, my desire to help smart entrepreneurs, inventors and scientists to create and commercialize products and technologies that can not only generate profits, but that can also make the world a better place. I believe you get what you give in life; if society benefits through my investments, society will reciprocate. Good always begets good.

My style of investing is called impact investing, which is meant to provide capital to "companies, organizations and funds with the intention to generate social and environmental impact alongside a financial return," as described in the 2017 Annual Impact Investor Survey released by the Global Impact Investing Network.

Impact investing is why I invested in the development of a bio-artificial liver device after my mother passed away from liver failure at age 57. As I said earlier, losing my mother not only put me into a deep depression, it was also devastating for our entire family. Her passing was the catalyst that motivated me to try and help save others from the same illness. You can read more about this part of my life in chapter 10.

It's also why I invested, and now have controlling positions, in two innovative publicly traded companies that are, to borrow from Warren Buffet, my two great ideas.

The first is SolarWindow, which has developed transparent coatings that turn ordinary windows into electricity-generating windows (www.solarwindow.com), for which the possibilities and benefits to society, in my opinion, may be endless.

The second public company is RenovaCare (www.renovacareinc.com), which has developed the SkinGun™ to spray a patient's skin stem cells onto severe burns and wounds. Again, in my opinion, the potential benefit to society warranted my investment.

My style of investing is also why I have written this book. My goal is to share the strategies that have worked so well in my life, strategies that have allowed my team and me to generate double-digit returns (45 percent per year annualized since 2006), in both good markets and bad.

By sharing my hard-earned knowledge with all those interested, my goal is to help others many as others have helped me. If just one individual benefits from the information in this book, hopefully you or someone you know, then I've accomplished my goal.

2 | JUMP ON THE POPULATION GROWTH WAVE

The U.S. is growing by 1 person every 18 seconds.

Over the years, I have invested in many companies, both public and private, ranging from old-tech auto salvage to new-tech enterprises companies that included an early version of Angie's List and Robinhood, the online brokerage firm launched in 2014.

However, despite the potential for significant personal and financial rewards, this style of investing also involves substantial risks. So, in 2006, I established Talia Jevan Properties (www.taliajevan.com) to provide relatively low-risk (remember, all investments have associated risks) investment diversity. As ongoing cash-flow has always been important to me, I stayed away from development and value-add projects, which require skills and acumen that I still need to acquire.

So, to minimize my risk exposure, I focused on the ownership of high-quality, full or almost full commercial properties in cities with economic strength, stability and a variety of income streams (technology, tourism, industry, etc.), social and cultural diversity, geographical appeal and, most importantly, population growth.

According to the U.S. Census Bureau, one baby is born about every 8 seconds, versus one death every 10 seconds. Add the net migration of 1 person every 31 seconds and you have a country that is now growing by one person every 18 seconds (as at February 25th, 2019). In comparison, Australia and Canada are each growing by one person every 75 seconds, while Germany is growing by one person every 4 minutes. In case you're wondering, China and India are adding 1 person every 6 seconds and 2 seconds respectively.

In 1960, there were almost 200 million people in the United States. By the end of 2018, the population had grown to nearly 330 million. All of these people must live somewhere, must work somewhere and must relax somewhere. This burgeoning population is why neighborhoods

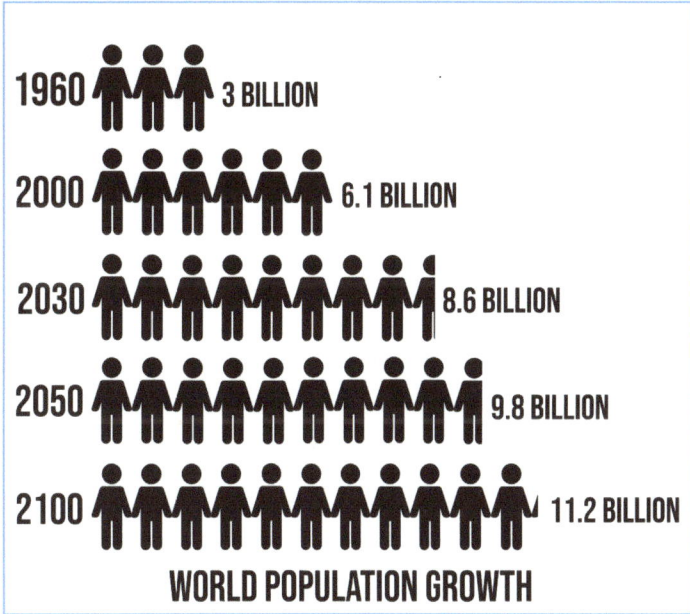

1960 3 BILLION

2000 6.1 BILLION

2030 8.6 BILLION

2050 9.8 BILLION

2100 11.2 BILLION

WORLD POPULATION GROWTH

Source: The World Bank.

are gentrifying all across the U.S., from Seattle's South Lake Union area to Boyle Heights in Los Angeles and all the way across to Brooklyn, NY, where Williamsburg is all the rage. In the years to come, new buildings will be built right next to existing buildings, which, all things being equal, will only go up in value due to increased demand just to accommodate the growing population.

As recently as 2007, an area called Gastown in Vancouver had a tattered reputation, known for its homelessness, panhandlers and drug dealers. Just five years later, in 2012, Complex, a New York fashion magazine, ranked Gastown as the fourth most stylish neighborhood in the world, right behind New York's SoHo, Tokyo's Harajuku and, the neighborhood judged the world's most stylish, the first arrondissement in Paris.

From Gastown in Vancouver, down to the Gaslamp Quarter in San Diego and all the way across the continent to the Meatpacking District in New York, entire sections of previously shunned areas are becoming popular as the growing population encroaches on available buildings, many of which are being renovated, modernized and repurposed. In Vancouver, for example, the original Vancouver Stock Exchange (where I delivered as a messenger in my early days) is now a hotel and office tower.

This phenomenon is also occurring in cities across the planet, where the population has gone from around 3 billion in 1960 to a current 7.6 billion, according to the United Nations. As a result, some areas of Berlin, London, Barcelona and even Panama's Casco Viejo are almost unrecognizable from only a few years ago.

Despite declining fertility rates in nearly all regions of the world, this growth in population is not slowing. By 2030, just 11 years from now, the world population is expected to increase by a staggering 1 billion people. By 2050, there will be 9.8 billion people in total. Again, all these people must live somewhere, work somewhere and relax somewhere.

H A R M E L   S .   R A Y A T

"Ninety percent of all millionaires become so through owning real estate," once said Andrew Carnegie. "More money has been made in real estate than in all industrial investments combined. The wise young man or wage earner of today invests his money in real estate."

Of course, and Andrew Carnegie's sentiment notwithstanding, it's important to point out that even though my team and I attempt to minimize our risk exposure, an investment in real estate can be risky. In fact, there are any number of factors, or risks, that can significantly and adversely affect your return on a real estate investment. These risks generally include, to name a few, changes in economic conditions, tenant defaults or ongoing vacancies, increases in interest and mortgage rates, availability of financing on favorable terms, environmental and zoning laws and illiquidity.

Another risk factor is knowledge or, more specifically, the lack thereof. When I acquired my first property in 2006, I had virtually no knowledge of real estate investing, not even having an understanding of the most commonly used valuation metric called the capitalization rate.

Understanding of capitalization rates and other essential factors aside, even before I made my first real estate acquisition, my intent was to treat everyone fairly, respectfully and with complete integrity, including sales and leasing agents, lawyers, various vendors, bankers and, most importantly, my valued tenants; I wanted to follow the Golden Rule: "Do unto others as you would have them do unto you."

3 TIMING VERSUS LOCATION

One of the most important lessons I have ever learned.

Bob Levine, a close friend, a valued mentor and someone I hold in the highest of regard, once told me something I will never forget: "Harmel, everyone thinks that it is location, location, location when it comes to real estate investing. Well, it's not! It is timing, timing, timing." This has been one of the most critical real estate lessons that I have ever learned.

Bob Levine is not only the co-founder of Avison Young, which has approximately 5,000 employees and 125 offices worldwide, but he is also a genuinely sincere and kind individual who freely shares his hard-earned knowledge and experiences. Listening to him and learning from him is like digging into a solid vein of gold; it's priceless.

While location is important indeed, an even more important factor is timing. Timing doesn't just necessarily mean buying assets at deep discounts during the Great Recession, a generational opportunity, it can also mean just being there with cash in hand to pay a fair price to acquire a high-quality property.

Sometimes, timing can actually mean paying a premium today rather than waiting to buy a high-quality, well-located building in a thriving area with a growing population, which generally means that lease rates can be increased over time. This is the strategy I employed when I bought the Leckie Building in Gastown back in June 2006 for just under $18 million, which was $4.5 million more than the institutional seller paid less than a year prior. I then spent an additional $1.5 million doing the various upgrade discussed in chapter 7.

In January 2016, the Leckie Building was independently appraised for almost $50 million. By mid-2018, it was worth about 5-times what I originally paid (see photo on page 19).

Timing can also mean not buying when new competing properties are coming online or when the cost of new construction is lower than market prices, which granted doesn't happen very often. New construction costs are generally rising, which means you can acquire a decent building in the midst of a lot of development and offer a great product at a lower price and still do quite well.

Timing can mean having cash available and being able to move fast when others can't, as Warren Buffett has been known to do. You need a great location with great nearby amenities to be sure, but without the right timing, you've lost before you've even had a chance to start. As Baron Rothschild once said, "The way to make money is to buy when blood is running in the streets." I would add that the best way to make money is when blood is running and when someone needs the cash in a hurry.

Trump Entertainment Resorts originally paid $282 million for its casino and hotel in New Jersey—a great location without a doubt, but the timing was off. In 2011, Tilman Fertitta of Landry's restaurant fame bought the same waterfront complex from Trump for $38 million, just under 15 percent of what Trump paid.

You could have bought the best house on the best corner in 2007, only to find your investment collapse in value by 40 percent in 2009. So much for location! The time to have bought that house was after the 2008 crash. By the way, according to Trulia, as of mid-2017 only about one-third of U.S. homes have surpassed their pre-recession peak values. Not surprisingly, the markets that have recovered are the ones with economic strength and social and geographical appeal resulting in employment and population growth, such as Denver, Seattle and San Francisco, to name just a few.

In his 2014 shareholder letter, here's how Warren Buffett addressed the importance of timing:

> "The when is also important. In 1993, I made another small investment. Larry Silverstein, Salomon's landlord when I was the company's CEO, told me about a New York retail property adjacent to New York University that the Resolution Trust Corporation (RTC) was selling. Again, a bubble had popped—this one involving commercial real estate—and the RTC had been created to dispose of the assets of failed savings institutions whose optimistic lending practices had fueled the folly.

> "Here too the analysis was simple: The unleveraged current yield from the property was about 10 percent. But the property had been under managed by the RTC, and its income

The Leckie Building is in Gastown, once a rough area but now amongst the most stylish neighborhoods in the world.

would increase when several vacant stores were leased. Even more important, the largest tenant—who occupied around 20 percent of the project's space—was paying rent of about $5 per foot, whereas other tenants averaged $70. The expiration of this bargain lease in nine years was certain to provide a major boost to earnings. The property's location was also superb: NYU wasn't going anywhere.

"As old leases expired, earnings tripled. Annual distributions now exceed 35 percent of our initial equity investment. Moreover, our original mortgage was refinanced in 1996 and again in 1999, moves that allowed several special distributions totaling more than 150 percent of what we had invested."

4 ALWAYS BE FAIR

You're not getting a Rolls Royce for the price of a Mercedes.

Just like everyone, I like buying quality merchandise at marked down prices. Unfortunately, high-quality, well-located real estate with in-place cash flow from great tenants and upside capital appreciation potential over time rarely comes at a discount.

Absent a once-in-a-generation event such as the Great Recession or when the RTC was selling assets of savings and loan associations, with high-quality commercial or residential real estate, you will only ever get these properties for a fair price, not a discounted price. You are not getting a Rolls Royce for the price of a Mercedes.

The kind of "sleep at night" real estate I seek to acquire does not come with a bargain-basement sticker price, only a fair price, a price that a prudent seller would accept. If a property can be had on the cheap, there is a reason. Maybe the roof is about to fail. Maybe seismic upgrading will soon be required. Maybe a major tenant has plans to move, maybe planned bike lanes will reduce parking and affect traffic patterns. Or, maybe a new nearby transit hub will change pedestrian flows. Whatever the reason, you're not getting a dollar for 75 cents.

While there are some in the industry who place great value in acquiring properties on a "price per pound" basis or a discount to what it cost to build, I believe the true economic value of a building is its ability to produce a return on investment. As an example, even if it cost $2 million to construct a property that generates $70,000 per year in net rental income, this property, all other things being equal, should have a market value of $1 million at a 7 percent capitalization rate.

To be fair, to buy a property for $10 million that cost $20 million to build has merit because it will be challenging for new buildings to compete, especially in areas undergoing gentrification or if a property has a specialty

My very first property was a 43,000 SF mixed-use building with beautiful water views and near schools, shopping and transportation.

use. Generally speaking though, it's likely that the building is selling for $10 million because the income being generated only values it at $10 million.

When I bought my very first building, I didn't nickel-and-dime the vendor, a fine old gentleman who had developed and held the property for a long time. Instead, I evaluated the asset based on what the property was yielding at the time, the quality of the building (which I confirmed by getting a property condition assessment or report), quality of the tenants (a national movie theatre was the main tenant), a thorough review of all leases and, lastly, the building's proximity to nearby amenities.

In this case, the building was in a great neighborhood, surrounded by apartment complexes, a school nearby and a short walk from a passenger-only ferry, seating 400 people, that departed every 15 minutes. With amazing water views, this building was also just blocks away from a major public market and a popular tourist attraction.

This was a no brainer to me, so I offered a price of almost $8 million, which was precisely what the seller felt his property was worth. Again, you are not getting a Rolls Royce for the price of a Mercedes. He sold me the building versus someone else because I recognized the value he had created and offered him a fair price for a fantastic property.

While others might have thought I paid too much, six years later, I sold the building for a $3 million profit. I sold because I was concerned about how Netflix might impact the movie theatre, which, as it turned out, ended up not renewing their lease.

The new owners of the property now have plans to develop a high-rise apartment building on the site, which I am sure is because of the magnificent water views and all the nearby amenities. The good news about real estate is that it can be very forgiving of mistakes and miscalculations, especially if you hold on for the long term. I am sure the new owners of my first building will do fine over time.

London's Canary Wharf and even the Empire State Building were both thought to be expensive propositions initially, yet eventually they turned into big money makers for smart, patient investors.

Contrary to many who nickel-and-dime with lowball bids, I am happy to present fair and respectful offers for high-quality, unimpaired assets, which I did with my very first acquisition and continue to do to this day.

Paying fair prices for quality assets and then focusing on providing five-star service at fair and reasonable rental rates is indeed lucrative, especially when the population in the U.S. and elsewhere is increasing day by day.

5 | FOLLOW THE GOLDEN RULE

You will never get heat from a fireplace without first putting in the wood.

While an experienced property manager might keep your building glistening and operating smoothly, there is one task he or she cannot perform: treating your tenants and everyone else associated with your property following the Golden Rule. Most property managers have multiple clients, so they couldn't possibly visit and spend quality time with your tenants regularly, which is what my team and I routinely do with ours.

Near the tail end of 2006, I mentioned to an asset manager of a multi-billion dollar institutional investor that I wanted to treat everyone, including agents, bankers and especially my tenants, with appreciation and sincere gratitude. I said, "this is exactly the way a luxury hotelier treats their guests—with respect and courtesy." When I got to the part about taking my tenants to luncheons and dinners, he almost burst out laughing. He said to me, "No one does that!"

However, in my mind, paying careful attention to our tenants is just as critical as providing electricity and water to our properties. When tenants know that you sincerely care, and genuinely treat them well, they'll happily pay their rents on time, renew their leases with joy and become your best source of referrals for new tenants.

In fact, the majority of our tenants don't think of our buildings as just an expense item on their income statement or just a place to work. Instead, most of our tenants regard our exceptional properties as essential tools they use to attract and retain quality staff, to proudly invite their clients to visit and to generate healthy profits over time.

Likewise, my team and I don't think of our properties as just buildings in a portfolio, the way many institutional investors do. Rather, we regard our properties the same way as the Four Seasons and the Ritz-Carlton think of theirs—as FIVE-star assets. And, just like these leading luxury hotel operators, we're all about providing exceptional service.

Our buildings are always maintained at the highest level, from immaculately clean restrooms and hallways and superbly maintained landscaping rivaling most resort hotels to having someone available to speak on a moment's notice. For us, it's all about service. As Earl Nightingale once said, "the greater your service, the greater your rewards." You'll never get heat from a fireplace without first putting in the wood; the wood is the service and the heat is the reward.

My team and I offer excellent service and impeccably maintained premises at fair and reasonable prices. This is why we consistently receive sincere praise from our many tenants, which is as rare as the four-leaf clover. Can you recall the last time you heard of a tenant speaking well of their landlord?

In the almost 15 years that I have proudly owned commercial real estate, I have yet to see any other institutional sized landlord receive the kind of accolades we do.

Here are just a few of our many tenant testimonials:

"As a large school, we have been tenants of many landlords, and we can confidently say that

Talia Jevan is one of the best landlords (if not the best) we have ever dealt with. They provide genuine excellence in service to their tenants."

—Razi S.

"We've leased thousands of square feet of commercial office space through the years from both institutional partners as well as various "ma and pa" landlords, and I can honestly say no one was better to work with than the team at Talia Jevan from start-to-finish."

—Dave B.

"From the gentleman who greets us at the door in the morning to maintenance, management and ownership, we have been made to feel absolutely welcome, appreciated and at home. I could not overstate my assertion that there is not a landlord anywhere as awesome as this group. I would be happy to give a direct reference to anyone interested."

—Mark M.

"I could go on about the exemplary condition of the heritage building we inhabit, or the outstanding service provided us by the staff at Talia Jevan Properties (all of which are true) but what really sets Harmel and his team apart, is hospitality. Harmel's ability to make each and every tenant feel like family creates a culture of trust and peace of mind. It's as if his entire team subscribe to a mentality that the tenant's happiness is their responsibility and they really do make you feel appreciated."

—Nick R.

Talia Jevan Properties and their management team have always added a personal touch to this property that you don't usually get from land-lords of properties this size. They have worked closely with us to ensure that the grounds stay clean and well-maintained and to ensure that all of our needs as a tenant are met. They were also essential in helping facilitate our restaurant's patio expansion which has helped increase revenues significantly."

—John B.

For additional video testimonials, please visit our web-site at www.taliajevan.com.

No matter how large or small the tenant, we have treated everyone the same way, following the Golden Rule. One company, Global Relay, started out with a modest 2,500-square-foot office in 2005 in one of our buildings. By 2016, and now with offices in New York,

Chicago, Raleigh, London, Singapore and London, this tenant had become a global technology leader and was occupying 62,000 square-feet in the same building. Over a period of 10 years, working in collaboration with Colin Scarlett from Colliers International, we worked hard to accommodate their needs 10 times in the same building.

"Because of our business friendly partnership with our landlord, we have been able to expand our business globally from one of the world's most beautiful cities, in one of Western Canada's most accommodating, attractive, and well-serviced buildings," said Kelvin Ng, Director of Business Operations at Global Relay. "Mr. Rayat has made it possible for us to expand our office space when we needed to, ensuring we can continue to grow."

In any transaction, when your guiding principle is to deal fairly, honestly and transparently, both sides win. When you treat tenants with respect and care, your whole real estate business improves significantly. In addition to existing tenants staying longer, you don't incur expenses finding new tenants, you enjoy higher occupancy rates, and your net operating income goes up. Most importantly, you develop warm, lasting relationships with your existing tenants. Over the years, many of my tenants, including Jim Falconer, Rob King and Kelvin Ng, all of whom I admire and respect immensely, have become great friends of mine.

With soaring ceilings and a grand staircase, this property is on a prime corner near many amenities and a stone's throw from the ocean.

Because of our excellent service, our sincere regard for our tenants and, again, our guiding philosophy of always dealing fairly, the vast majority of our many leases have taken at most a few hours in total time to consummate. While hard to comprehend by most in the industry, my current record time stands at a mere 15 minutes for a 5-year renewal that involved a substantial increase in rent and under 10 minutes for a new lease with an existing tenant wishing to expand.

Our thinking is that when everything is fair, what is there to discuss? In fact, we don't need the very best deal to make us happy; we would rather have a fair deal so that everyone is happy.

One of our buildings is located on a prime downtown corner, with bus, ferry and train transportation minutes away. There are also numerous quality restaurants, hotels, top-notch shopping nearby and its a stone's throw from the ocean. What made this property truly unique was its expansive floor plate, soaring ceilings and grand "Gone with the Wind" staircase similar to the one at the Jefferson Hotel, where everyone from Elvis and The Rolling Stones to George W. Bush and Barack Obama have stayed.

With a 20,000-square-foot lease renewal fast approaching and nothing comparable in the city, my tenant and I were in a quandary as to how to come up with a renewal rate. Wanting to be fair and reasonable, as always, I suggested that we retain an independent party to prepare a report and arrive at a fair per-square-foot rate rather than going the traditional way of being represented by leasing agents. I gave my tenant the opportunity of choosing their own consultant so that there would be no question of independence. I said that I would not only pay for the report, but I would also happily accept whatever rate was deemed to be reasonable by the consultant of their choosing.

This sophisticated tenant, with locations across North America, instead asked us to choose the consultant. Right after the report's completion, we both agreed to the recommendation of the consultant—this despite renewal rates that were almost double the existing rates! Everyone was happy because the transaction was fair all around. Given the unique structure of the building and its location to great amenities, it's possible that we could have pushed for higher rates, but we didn't. Again, we don't need the very best deal to make us happy; we would rather have a fair deal so that everyone is happy.

Generally speaking, as long you own properties relatively close to desirable amenities in markets that have the requisite economic vitality and the social and geographical appeal to attract the growing population (that's why certain areas get more people moving in than other areas), you will be raising rents over time. However, despite this, there can be times when you have to lower rents and suffer the consequences of decreased cash flow and a lower property valuation as a result.

This happened to me when I made the classic "rookie" mistake of believing that the rates in the lease agreements represented fair market rent. Often, landlords will offer incentives to tenants in the form of free rent or other inducements while charging a relatively high "face" rate of rent, which is the primary driver for building valuations; the higher the face rent, the higher the valuation. In the case of free rent, the tenant enjoys rent abatement for a fixed period, making the true "effective" rental rate lower, oftentimes much lower.

In one medical building I bought, I thought I was getting a property with net market rental rates of $31.00 per square-foot (meaning the tenant pays for the operating expenses), but in actuality, the true market rate was closer to a gross of $24.50 per square-foot (meaning the landlord pays for the operating expenses). Upon various lease renewals at market rates, there was an immediate devaluation of my building by several million dollars, dropping my cash flow significantly. Ouch, that fiscally hurt! I go into more details about this and my other "rookie" mistakes in the next chapter.

The good news is that this medical building is near a major highway interchange, within both walking distance or a short drive from banking, numerous retail stores, bars and restaurants and several major hospitals. Just 3 miles away, is one of the busiest general aviation airports in all of the United States. Because people want to live and work near quality amenities, the value of my building will increase over time and I will eventually make up for the short-term drop in value and income.

Had Donald Trump held onto New York's Plaza Hotel, which he was forced to sell after taking on massive amounts of debt, he would be sitting on an asset worth substantially more today. As mentioned before, the wonderful aspect about real estate is that it can be very forgiving of mistakes, which you can't say for other asset classes. How many once dominant corporate names are now nothing more than a memory or a mere shell of their former glory?

In contrast, quality real estate holds its value and increases over time. That's why some of the most successful people in the world, people like Bill Gates, Larry Ellison and Michael Dell, not only hold massive amounts of real estate, but they continually buy new assets.

While visiting Houston in November 2018 to watch Kevin Durant of the Golden State Warriors play against James Harden's Houston Rockets, I learned that Bill Gates had just added the Four Seasons Hotel to his portfolio. Earlier in the same year, Michael Dell, through his family office, MSD Capital, acquired more than a dozen buildings in Dallas' Knox Street neighborhood for a reported $250 million.

6 | WHEN, WHERE AND HOW TO INVEST

How to generate relatively low-risk double-digit returns, in good markets and bad.

"Don't wait to buy real estate, buy real estate and wait," said T. Harv Eker. When you buy great properties and have a patient outlook, it's hard not to make money. That's why the Chinese say that the best time to have invested in real estate was 20 years ago; the second best time to invest is today!

Question: how do you know when to buy a great property?

Answer: when you can acquire a relatively low-risk, cash-producing, well-built and well-located asset between a 6 percent to 8 percent capitalization rate, it's always a good time to buy a property.

So that it's clear, the capitalization rate is the percentage obtained by dividing the net operating income produced by a building by the value of the building; the higher the capitalization rate, the lower the value of the property and vice versa.

If you invest at a 7 percent capitalization rate, for example, you'll double your money in about 10 years, at which time you will still have your property to sell based on a capitalization rate of your net operating income of the property at that time. Since net operating income generally rises over time, so will the value of your property!

I chose to invest in office properties because they generally have higher capitalization rates than residential, while industrial properties usually have higher capitalization rates than office. Also, generally speaking, higher capitalization rates correspond with higher risk assets, while lower rates are associated with lower risk assets. In Vancouver, where I live, apartment properties are changing hands at capitalization rates of between 2 percent and 3 percent. In other gateway cities, such as Boston or

New York, the capitalization rates of office properties are currently between 4 percent and 5 percent.

When choosing a market for yourself, choose one that has diverse economic drivers, financial stability, social and geographic appeal and, most importantly, population growth, which, in my opinion, has no ending in sight, especially in the U.S., which is growing by 1 person every 18 seconds.

If you're wondering where you can acquire a quality asset producing 7 percent (plus or minus a point or two), they're available in many cities. I chose to invest in Phoenix, the 5th largest and one of the fastest growing cities in the United States. Phoenix also rates among the most desirable communities in the nation, with a year-round average temperature of 75 degrees Fahrenheit.

Here are a few other fast growing cities in America, as reported by USA Today:

Dallas-Fort Worth-Arlington, Texas:
- 2010-2017 pop. growth: +14.7 percent (from 6,451,833 to 7,399,662)
- 2010-2017 pop. change due to migration: +555,586
- Largest 12-month change: +152,393 (2015-2016)
- Median household income: $63,812

Raleigh, North Carolina:
- 2010-2017 pop. growth: +17.4 percent (from 1,137,393 to 1,335,079)
- 2010-2017 pop. change due to migration: +139,611
- Largest 12-month change: +32,021 (2015-2016)
- Median household income: $71,685

Orlando-Kissimmee-Sanford, Florida:
- 2010-2017 pop. growth: +17.3 percent (from 2,139,317 to 2,509,831)
- 2010-2017 pop. change due to migration: +291,358
- Largest 12-month change: +63,099 (2014-2015)
- Median household income: $52,385

Boise City, Idaho:
- 2010-2017 pop. growth: +14.9 percent (from 617,980 to 709,845)
- 2010-2017 pop. change due to migration: +62,059
- Largest 12-month change: +19,035 (2016-2017)
- Median household income: $55,162

Bend-Redmond, Oregon:
- 2010-2017 pop. growth: +18.5 percent (from 157,740 to 186,875)
- 2010-2017 pop. change due to migration: +26,052
- Largest 12-month change: +6,387 (2015-2016)
- Median household income: $61,870

By way of a very simple example (using pre-tax numbers and assuming no debt), let's say you acquire a quality commercial office property for $2,000,000 at a 7 percent capitalization rate which has various lease agreements with staggering expirations and 3 percent annual rent increases. This means that your year 1 income of $140,000 (dividing $140,000 by 7 percent is how you arrive at a $2,000,000 valuation) would increase to $182,668.25 by year 10, providing a total income of $1,604,943.10 over 10 years.

At year 10, and again assuming 7 percent capitalization rate, your property would be worth $2,609,546.37, which works out to an annualized relatively low-risk return of 11 percent (simple interest), without the volatility and gut-wrenching gyrations of the stock market. In comparison, the current yield on a 10-year bond is less than 3 percent. At maturity, all you get back is your principal, which will likely have less buying power due to inflation.

In addition to the tax benefits of depreciation, there are other ways to boost your real estate returns further still, such as adding mortgage financing and renewing leases that come due every few years at higher prices. There's also the possibility of selling at a lower capitalization rate due to higher demand, which will increase the value of your building. Combined, these factors could easily send your absolute returns upwards of 20 percent on a relatively low-risk basis.

By way of comparison, the annualized return for the S&P 500 Index for the 10 years ended December 31, 2018, was 13 percent. Longer term, for the 20 years ended December 31, 2018, the return was just 8 percent, which is closer to the long-term annual norm.

I started investing in real estate in 2006 without any previous experience. By doing exactly what I am sharing with you in this book, my team and I have generated annualized returns of 45 percent per year for the 13 years ended December 31, 2018. This is 3 times better than the NASDAQ market and 5 times better than the Dow over the same period. Had I known what I know now, I would have jumped into real estate much sooner.

Remember, again, the U.S. is growing by one person every 18 seconds. More than twice as many people are born every day than the number that die throughout the world. All these people have to live somewhere, work somewhere and play somewhere! However, this growing population is not settling evenly across the country.

According to the Washington Post, 50 percent of the U.S. population lives in the country's 144 largest counties, with 39 percent of the population in counties that

RETURNS PER YEAR
SINCE 2006

45%	TALIA JEVAN

7.5% S&P 500 **8.9%** DOW JONES **9.4%** FTSE NAREIT **15%** NASDAQ **45%** TALIA JEVAN

ANNUALIZED RETURNS FOR TALIA JEVAN PROPERTIES FOR THE 13 YEARS ENDED DECEMBER 31, 2018.

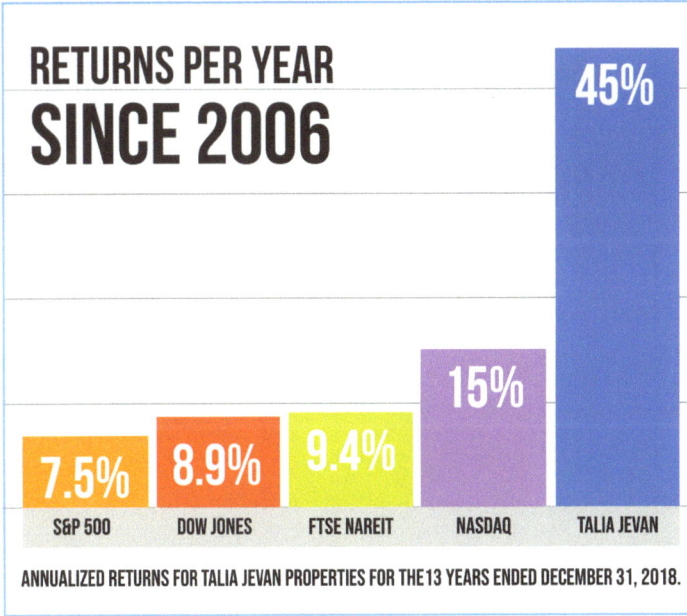

are directly adjacent to an open ocean, a major estuary or the Great Lakes. The balance lives in the smaller 2,998 counties. So, after you have decided which city you want to invest in, you must then determine precisely where in that city your property will be located. Here, I suggest you follow the old 80/20 rule and invest in that 20 percent of the city where 80 percent of the people want to be. You'll be glad you did.

Most people prefer to work in a market where job growth is robust, varied and growing. So, before investing in any property, whether residential or commercial, make sure it's in a populated, growing region and check on nearby amenities. People want to live close to transit, schools, shopping, health care providers, parks and other recreational facilities.

Since many first-time real estate investors have modest or average means to acquire quality buildings, whether residential or commercial, I am often asked how a regular individual starts out. My simple response: do what people have been doing from time immemorial and get help from family and friends.

If you don't have adequate funds on hand, ask a few friends to join you in a partnership, just like Harry Helmsley did—he had several thousand! It won't take long to rustle up $200,000, $400,000, $600,000 or much more as most people are desperate for the high, relatively low-risk returns that high-quality properties generate.

Immigrant families have been banding together to buy real estate for generations. Heck, even Donald Trump had help from his father, as did Ray Dalio during the early days of Bridgewater Associates. And, it can be lucrative for all concerned. Harry Helmsley's Empire State Building limited partnership, for example, has created hundreds of limited partner millionaires over the years.

Another question I get asked is "How do I look after my building?" The answer to this is also simple: hire a property manager. For a modest monthly fee, there are

The Optum Building serves as a regional headquarter for a Fortune 10 company and has a number of other prominent medical practices.

plenty of professional managers who will take care of all the day-to-day details of maintaining and managing a building, including collecting rent, paying bills, generating financial statements and producing annual budgets. From when I first started and to this very day, I still rely on third-party property managers, as do most out-of-country, out-of-state and out-of-city real estate owners. Perhaps this explains why the global property management market is a $14.5 billion industry?

Excellent property management notwithstanding, over the years I have made quite a few rookie mistakes that you, as a neophyte real estate investor, need not make if you keep your eyes open. One of the oldest tricks in the book is to offer incentives to tenants to lease out properties.

However, these incentives are not typically reflected in (or deducted from) "face" rental rates. Smart landlords, wanting to maintain high building valuations, will do their very best to keep their face rental rates high. The higher the rental rate, the higher the valuation of the property. So, they typically end up paying for the incentives themselves.

For example, a landlord may have induced a tenant with free rent for a specific time frame or provided an above-market tenant improvement allowance. As you'll discover later in this chapter, existing tenant improvements are mostly of value to incumbent tenants. Let's take an example of a 5-year lease for a 2,500-square-foot office at an annual rental rate of $15 per square-foot. By providing 10 months of rental abatement, the face rate of the $15 per square-foot lease becomes a $12.50 net effective rate, which is generally speaking the rate I use for valuation purposes. The lesson here is that you want to obtain details of any lease inducements offered in the building you acquire, and compare these to the rental rates of nearby comparable buildings. You'll very quickly discover what the actual market rates are so you don't make the mistakes I have made.

As mentioned in chapter 5, I bought a medical building (see photo on page 47) with in-place rental rates of $31.00 per square-foot net for a large portion of the building, but in actuality, the market rates were around $24.50 per square-foot gross. When the leases were renewed at the lower market rents, there was an immediate devaluation of my building by several million dollars. However, with national credit tenants, including a Fortune 10 company that uses this building as a regional headquarter, a prominent and highly regarded cardiology group headed by Dr. John Raniolo, and several other leading medical practices, the cash-flow remained strong and will increase over time, as will the value of the building as rents bump up annually.

There are some building owners, I call them "lipstick and bubble gum" landlords, who try to squeeze out as much income out of a property as possible. These types of landlords prefer to stretch out routine maintenance schedules, paint over or patch up instead of repairing or replacing and generally do not invest much back into their building. This is where obtaining an expert property condition assessment or report by a reputable firm will come in handy prior to any purchase. A small amount of money spent upfront pinpointing where all the hidden problems are could save you a whole lot of expensive misery in the future. Of course, the cost of any deferred maintenance you discover during your due diligence should be deducted from the purchase price of any property you decide to acquire.

Another trap for newbie landlords, including myself, is assuming that existing tenant improvements have residual value after an incumbent tenant leaves. In the vast majority of the cases, this is not so. Back in the 1990s, to build my personal office, I retained the services of renowned architect Timothy Bullinger, designer of quality projects all around the world, from Beverly Hills to Shenzhen. Timothy designed a beautiful suite of offices for my team and me, with custom millwork throughout, exquisite use of stone and large panes of glass that were so heavy they had to be craned in.

Sadly, when I eventually sold my strata office space to move into larger premises in my own building, the new owner ripped most of these improvements out, causing tears to well up in my eyes.

The medical building that I mentioned earlier had many tenants, including one that had spent a significant amount of money installing a surgery center, complete with nursing stations and a number of beds for overnight stays and patient recovery. When this tenant left, the next one trashed all of the expensive improvements, causing even more tears to well up in my eyes. So, remember that most existing tenant improvements have little, if any, value to anyone else. Don't let anyone tell you otherwise.

Seeking higher returns or cheaper property prices, or both, many people get lured into smaller towns and areas on the outskirts of where the action is. While they might enjoy a bit higher yield going in, remember that when it comes time to re-lease the premises or sell their building, the number of prospects for an out-of-the-way location is a lot less. So, their property might sit empty or unsold for a while. Again, stick to the 80/20 rule and only buy properties in the 20 percent of the community where 80 percent of the people want to be. However, and remembering the rate of population growth over time, the small towns of today will be the big towns of tomorrow.

When commercial properties have less than the desired amount of parking available to accommodate the needs of tenants and their customers and guests, you will often hear people talk about the impact that Uber, Lyft, Waymo and eventually other autonomous vehicle brands will have on parking. The consensus is that less and less parking space will be needed in the years to come. Until this happens, if it happens, I would recommend buying properties that have plenty of in-place parking. In the future, if there is indeed less parking space needed, you will have the opportunity of selling the extra land or perhaps developing a new building on the unused property yourself; what an excellent way to land-bank.

Finally, remember that it takes time to build value in an asset. In fact, and as memorialized in one of Aesop's Fables about the tortoise and the hare, the slower you go, the faster you get there. So, don't expect to sell for big profits in a short period of time; although this happens on occasion, it is one of the fallacies embraced by many in the business.

7 | AVOID AS MUCH RISK AS POSSIBLE

It's better to get rich slowly than going broke fast.

If you think of any individual property as a small business, real estate development is the equivalent of starting a new business. Moreover, since 80 percent of new small businesses fail within 18 months, according to Forbes, real estate development by its very nature is risky. In contrast, buying a commercial property with current tenants and an in-place net operating income is the equivalent of purchasing an already established business, so the success rate is much higher.

Installing water features, improving landscaping and adding accent lighting are among the many ways of enhancing the appeal of a property.

In my opinion, it's better to get rich slowly than going broke fast by taking on too much risk, which in real estate includes taking on too much debt. This is why, contrary to popular opportunistic or developmental real estate strategies, which often involve lots of risk and debt, my team and I focus on getting the highest returns with the lowest risk profile. As a result, and because I am risk averse with my real estate investments, we only buy high-quality properties in growing and thriving areas that are close to great amenities and have great tenants with leases of varying duration.

I also avoid opportunistic investments because it's hard to consistently come by genuinely good opportunities. There is always a "real" reason why a building is empty or impaired, which is not often the reason the vendor or real estate agent shares during the sales process. In fact, I have never been tempted to buy a run-down commercial property, gut it and turn the building into condos for a profit, for example. If the opportunity was that simple or easy, the vendor would have done it instead of selling out or perhaps even partnered with an experienced developer, of which there are many.

Real estate development is another challenging arena. To be clear, while there are huge profits to be made in development, it is a very high-risk business and requires years and years of specialized experience. While many developers do very well, many also file for bankruptcy.

Some time back, I was asked to provide the equity capital for the development of a large lakefront resort project. After some reflection and independent advice from a highly regarded real estate lawyer, Murray Braaten, I respectfully declined. You see, among many other things, as I was told, if the projections are off by even a tiny bit, your expected profits can evaporate quickly.

As it turned out, and is often the case, the developers of the lakefront venture miscalculated and missed their sales projections. While I am sure they will eventually do well, it's going to take longer for them to reach their anticipated goals.

Another way to reduce risk, and the risk of losing tenants to other buildings, is to enhance the physical appeal of your property by continually reinvesting in your asset. This can be done in many ways, cheap and not so cheap. Among the many ways to improve a building are to upgrade bathrooms, install accent lighting, improve landscaping, add music to lobbies and elevators, paint before needing to, polish brass and other fixtures and install bike lockers, showers and other building amenities. Generally speaking, you want to keep your building in pristine condition.

Additionally, my team and I try our very best to operate our buildings as cost efficiently as possible by actively pursuing cost-reduction initiatives, such as engaging property tax appeal specialists to lower property taxes and implementing energy savings programs. For example, in one of my buildings, we upgraded the lights in the common areas, elevators, bathrooms and stairwells, to LED, which lowered the electricity costs. In the future, I envision utilizing other new technologies, such as electricity-generating windows (see chapter 10) to reduce electricity costs in my buildings.

Perhaps the best way to avoid risk is to be mindful of the amount of mortgage debt you take on. I have always viewed debt like salt: too much is no good and too little is no good. As a result, I have kept my debt levels to no

Among the smaller of my buildings, this mortgage-free property generates better cashflow than assets many times larger.

higher than 65 percent of the value of the property value upon acquisition. Over time, as I have raised rents and my property values have gone up, my mortgage debt as a percentage of my total portfolio value has gone down substantially, allowing me to refinance and invest in additional assets, a strategy employed by many in real estate. One long-term property owner I know of has built a portfolio approaching $1.5 billion by never having sold a single property, preferring instead to refinance on occasion to free up equity to reinvest.

A few years ago, I was asked to moderate a panel of real estate investment trust (REIT) professionals in Las Vegas before an audience of about 500 investors, all eager to hear what the panelists had to say and to ask questions of various sorts. The panel consisted of a number of experienced and very smart individuals, each representing a REIT holding billions of dollars in real estate assets for their respective organizations.

Of all the questions asked that day, one in particular stood out in my mind. It came from somewhere in the back of the room and was directed at a panel member whose organization did not mortgage their assets; all of their property acquisitions were made with cash. If any properties have existing debt, they immediately pay it off. This was the first time I had been exposed to this type of investment strategy and it intrigued me so much that I asked the panel member after the session was over why they did not have debt. "We don't have debt because we prefer to keep 100 percent of the profits from our hard work versus giving most of it away to the banks," he said.

I went back to examine the financial statements of my various buildings and what I saw shocked me. On every property I owned that had a mortgage, my bankers had been making more than I every year, in some cases substantially more. And, on a small property that I didn't have mortgage debt on, it was producing more cashflow than buildings four times its size.

Massive family fortunes, from the Rothschilds to the Medicis, have been made in banking and lending. To this day, banks are generating record profits year after year because lending money is so very lucrative. How lucrative, you may ask? Well, let's take a simple example of a $500,000 mortgage (30-year amortization at 6 percent interest) taken out on January 1, 2019. By January 1, 2020, a year later, you will have paid off only $6,700 in principal and paid almost $32,000 in interest. By January 1, 2023, your principal would have decreased by just $27,500, while your interest paid would be close to $120,000, more than 4 times the principal you worked so hard to pay down.

In 10 years, you will have paid down only $72,000 of the principal and paid $255,000 in interest charges, more than half of what you borrowed originally. And, all this while, the mortgage holder, the bank or whoever, will have true ownership of your property. Now you can see how profitable lending money can be. Perhaps this explains why Harry Helmsley raised so much equity from his limited partners ($33 million in equity as compared to a $6 million mortgage) when he bought the Empire State Building (see chapter 6).

Of course, the appropriate use of leverage may result in you committing significantly less of your own capital, which in turn enhances your ultimate return on capital investment. And, further, an argument can be made about the advantages of maximum leverage and the tax benefits of writing off the interest expense. But despite these advantages, many developers, from Harry Macklowe and Bruce Eicher to Donald Trump, have defaulted on loans after taking on too much debt.

Had I not purposely written this book at a high level for the sake of simplicity and sharing my strategies in an easy to understand and hopefully quick to implement way, I would go into more detail about this subject matter. I'll leave this for next time or perhaps a future blog post. In the meantime, I am working on reducing my own debt levels so that I, and not my bankers, can benefit from the extra money. I'd rather use this extra cash to acquire more assets, versus letting my bankers use it to lend out and make more money.

MY
S·U·C·C·E·S·S
FORMULA

8

After being broke several times, this formula has gotten me back on my feet each time.

Back in the 1980s, my older brother, Herdev S. Rayat, took me to a seminar about the Master Key System, which started me on a decades-long quest for personal development and self-improvement. Since then, I've read everything from Napoleon Hill and Earl Nightingale to Brian Tracy and Tony Robbins. I've combined the best of what these amazing people have to offer with lessons learned from other authors, lecturers, academicians and entrepreneurs to come up with an ever evolving and ever improving formula for success. This formula, which goes by the acronym SUCCESS, has helped me bounce back

1

from many personal and professional disasters. Today, I share the latest iteration.

Over the years, I have privately shared this formula with many individuals, ranging from young students wondering which careers to choose, to mature professionals wondering what to do with the careers they have already chosen. The remarkable thing about the SUCCESS formula is that it works every time, just like following any proven recipe. If you diligently follow a recipe for baking a particular type of cake, for example, you will get the same result whether you are in Tokyo, Toronto, Tampa, Turin, Tacoma or Toontown. However, to bake that delicious cake, each ingredient must be added at the precise moment, in the exact amount and then baked together for the prescribed period of time.

To be successful in business or your personal life, there is no ingredient more important than the first "S" in my SUCCESS formula, which stands for a sense of direction, a goal. You need a purpose in life to be fulfilled, both personally and professionally. If you don't, it's the same as floating around in a boat without a rudder, ending up wherever the tides of circumstance or the winds of the moment take you.

Before the engines are started, every airline pilot and ship captain knows exactly where he or she is headed.

Before each day begins, you also need to know where you're headed and which goals and opportunities you are pursuing. Sounds simple, yes? While most people will smile and nod in agreement, the statistics say otherwise. Shockingly, less than 3 percent of Americans have written goals, according to Brian Tracy. Moreover, only 1 person out of every 100 reviews and rewrites their goals daily.

"The beginning," as Plato once said, "is the most important part of any work." If you don't know where you are going, then any road will take you there, which explains why so many of us are so unfulfilled and in jobs we don't enjoy. However, there are the few among us that know exactly where they are headed. They are the 3 percent with written goals, who go from one success to another. So, start thinking carefully about your goals, which you should write down and then review daily.

It's also critical to focus on one single goal at a time, whether personal or professional. "Singleness of purpose," John D. Rockefeller once said, "is one of the chief essentials for success in life, no matter what may be one's aim." So do what Andrew Carnegie recommended back in 1885, "put all your eggs in one basket, and then watch that basket." Choose one single goal, and then throw all the energy you can muster into reaching that goal. Once you've achieved that goal, go onto the next one.

To reach your goal in the least amount of time, follow Earl Nightingale's strategy of working towards your goal "one day at a time." Before starting each day, list a half dozen tasks in the order of their importance for *that* day. Then, set to work on completing task #1, then task #2, task #3 and so on. Every single task completed puts you that much closer to reaching your goal. If a few tasks remain at the end of a day, no problem; complete them the next day.

Completing as many important tasks successfully each day results in a successful day. Five successful days results in a successful week. Four of these weeks become a successful month. In turn, twelve successful back-to-back months lead to a successful year. Before too long, all these successful years result in a successful career and a successful life.

The "U" in SUCCESS is for understanding. Once you have your sense of direction or chosen your goal, you need to amass the knowledge and the skills of how to get there. This step need not be so complicated or daunting. While you can learn and gain experience through your own hard work, of course, a far easier way is to learn through the hard work and hard-earned experience of others.

As mentioned in the introduction, if you want to learn how to play the piano, for example, find a great piano player to teach you. In my case, I wanted to learn how to scratch mix, so I sought out some of the best people around to learn from, people like DJ Hapa, DJ Chris Mac and DJ Revolution in Los Angeles. Learning from individuals that have spent years in school and decades climbing to the top of their chosen profession is like digging into a solid vein of gold. Tony Robbins calls this modeling, but make sure you are modeling the right people. There are too many poseurs on YouTube, Twitter, Instagram and elsewhere nowadays, so be very careful.

Figure out exactly what you need to learn, whether this involves going to university, going on YouTube or taking online courses. For many, reading books is the best way to learn, often from authors who have spent a lifetime accumulating specialized knowledge. By way of direct example, it took me decades to learn what I know and many months to distill my hard-earned know-how into an easy to understand format. By reading this book, you gain all my experience in just a few days; what a great way to learn and grow.

While knowledge is indeed power, it is also the greatest motivator in the world. With knowledge and understanding, the walls of ignorance eventually crumble as you move forward to your goal. However, you need to make sure you focus your energies to be truly effective. Don't be like the many who go through years of school learning skills that have nothing to do with the goal they end up pursuing. I know a doctor who decided to become a financier and a lawyer who decided to go into commercial real estate leasing.

"C" is for courage, another essential attribute on the road to success. Courage is not the absence of fear; courage is feeling the fear and doing it anyway, according to author Robert Gilbert. You must have the courage to leave the comfort of your daily life, surroundings and habits. You must have the courage to go against the grain. You must have the courage to weather the storm of critical comments that often come from naysayers, many of whom will be your friends and family.

As I know from personal experience (see chapter 10), many critics will hide behind the anonymity of the internet, gutlessly spewing their views and trying their best to tarnish your brand and your good reputation. Don't let this faze you or slow you down. "You just can't beat the person who never gives up," said Babe Ruth. So, resolve to have the courage to pick yourself up when you fail or when others are trying to knock you down, which will often happen if you're genuinely working on the outer edge of your potential.

Also, resolve to have the courage to move forward even if you lack in certain areas, as I did when I started in real estate in 2006 with no prior experience. The Wright brothers, before they made history at Kitty Hawk, "had no college education, no formal technical training, no experience working with anyone other than themselves, no friends in high places, no financial backers, no government subsidies, and little money of their own," as David McCullough wrote in his New York Times bestseller.

The second "C" in SUCCESS is for communication. Of all the skills to learn, one of the most important is the ability to clearly and persuasively communicate your thoughts and ideas. An article in Forbes stated, "It is simply impossible to become a great leader without being a great communicator." The Houston Chronicle reported: "No matter the size of your business, proficiency in oral and written communications is essential in promoting and maintaining a positive profile."

Throughout history, many of the world's most successful and most inspiring people have been powerful communicators. Whether it be David Meerman Scott, Jatinder S. Bhogal (with whom I have worked with for going on three decades), Winston Churchill or most any Fortune 500 CEO, all have outstanding communication skills.

"The one easy way to become worth 50 percent more than you are now—at least— is to hone your communication skills—both written and verbal," stated Warren

Buffett. So, make it a high priority to become a better orator and communicator, whether it be just to learn a new word every day or enroll in formal classes. Just do it.

"E" is for enthusiasm and excitement. When you believe in yourself, when you believe in your goals and are confident (not arrogant) in your expectations, you naturally exude an innate sense of enthusiasm that acts like a magnet, attracting others with a positive spirit as well. Before you know it, you'll be surrounded by like-minded individuals, all rooting for your success. Over time, your continued enthusiasm and positive energy will become infectious, attracting even more people still.

You have every reason to be enthusiastic and excited about your life. You are part of the elite 3 percent of the population that has written goals. You are following a time-tested strategy used by some of the most successful people in the world of working towards your goal one day at a time. Every day, you are completing the requisite tasks of only that day in the order of their importance. These completed tasks result in a successful day, which in turn leads to a successful week, a successful month, a successful year and eventually a successful life. This is exactly how a skyscraper is built—one day at a time. And, this is also how a successful life is built—one day at a time. So, make every day count!

The next "S" in SUCCESS is for self-discipline, which is essential to building life-changing habits. Michael Phelps got into the habit of spending thousands of hours staring at a black line at the bottom of a pool. In fact, for one five-year period, he trained every day, including twice on his birthday. He had the self-discipline to develop a daily swimming habit that made all the difference and resulted in him becoming the most decorated athlete in Olympic history.

An immediate reward for a lack of self-discipline is a day at the beach. A future reward of having self-discipline is owning that beach. Through self-discipline, you develop a daily habit of finishing important and critical tasks before meeting your friends to have fun or watch the game. Through self-discipline, you develop a habit of improving your communication skills rather than watching mind-numbing television or wasting hours on YouTube. Self-discipline leads to great habits, which invariably lead to success in life.

The final "S" is quite possibly the toughest for most: to start. Johann Wolfgang von Goethe said: "Whatever you can do or dream you can, begin it. Boldness has genius, power, and magic in it!" Many people "talk," but so few people "do."

To be sure, starting to work towards your written goal is very difficult, but remember the words of Lao-Tzu, who said, "A journey of a thousand miles begins with a single step." Should you find the first step difficult to take, remember that the best lesson that Richard Branson ever learned was to "just do it." All you have to do is "start," the most crucial ingredient in my SUCCESS formula.

9 | PUTTING IT ALL INTO PRACTICE

You'll never get to second base with one foot on first.

Now then, let's put what you learned in chapter 8 into practice. Let's say that your written goal is to buy a quality 10,000-square-foot multi-tenant commercial building located nearby amenities such as shopping, schools and restaurants and in a growing area with positive job growth from multiple types of employers (technology, manufacturing, biomedical, etc.). Because you want to double your money in about 10 years or so, on a relatively low-risk basis, you decide that you want to acquire an asset between a 6 percent and 8 percent capitalization rate.

Next, you go to work researching which market will offer you this kind of return, beginning with your own city before looking elsewhere. It's shocking how often the things we seek are right under our nose and in our very own backyard.

As also discussed in more detail in chapter 6, acquiring a well-kept and well-located $2,000,000 property with in-place leases that have 3 percent annual increases at a 7 percent capitalization rate, for example, could generate a relatively low-risk annualized simple rate of return of 11 percent per year over 10 years (assumes a 7 percent capitalization rate at year 10).

As illustrated on the next page, if you bought this same property for a 6 percent capitalization rate or an 8 percent capitalization rate, your annualized 10 year simple rate of return would vary slightly. However, if you have mortgage financing or the capitalization rate at year 10 is lower, or you consummate lease renewals at higher rates, your overall returns could easily top 15 percent, 20 percent or even much higher. By way of comparison, our in-house annualized returns have been 45 percent per year since 2006.

Once you have determined which market is best for you, make a point of meeting agents, appraisers, real estate lawyers, accountants and other professionals in that market to learn and understand as much as possible about expected

CAPITALIZATION RATE	6 PERCENT	7 PERCENT	8 PERCENT
BUILDING INCOME AT YEAR 1	$140,000	$140,000	$140,000
INITIAL BUILDING VALUE	$2,333,333	$2,000,000	$1,750,000
BUILDING INCOME AT YEAR 10	$182,668	$182,668	$182,668
BUILDING VALUE AT YEAR 10	$3,044,471	$2,609,546	$2,283,353
TOTAL 10 YEAR PRETAX INCOME	$1,604,943	$1,604,943	$1,604,943
ANNUALIZED RETURN (SIMPLE)	10% PER YEAR	11% PER YEAR	12% PER YEAR

If you add debt, have a lower capitalization rate at year 10 or sign leases at higher rates, your annualized returns could easily top 20 percent.

population growth rates, current and future economic drivers, building trends and other relevant factors. You will be surprised how much information you can gather just by speaking to people who have spent decades in the market you want to enter. Be honest and let these people know that you are looking to invest and that you're doing your homework first, which is precisely what I did when I started. It took me a while, but I was eventually able to meet some great people, who referred me to even more amazing people. Birds of a feather, truly do flock together!

Some of the agents you initially meet may actually be the same ones that start sending you acquisition targets. If not, get the names of the top agents in your area and ask to get onto to their email lists. In the blink of an eye, you'll be receiving many opportunities, most you will pass up but some you look at closer by signing a confidentiality agreement to access financial statements, building condition reports, appraisals and other information, which will

In 2013, I bought my first U.S. property for $16.5 million. It was a 74,000 SF mixed-use complex near the Mayo Clinic.

generally be rosy and positive. Remember, these real estate agents want to sell properties and earn a commission, so everything will always be "wonderful."

Although agents typically have pro-forma statements prepared for the commercial properties they are selling, I usually tend to create my own based on my assessment of what I think lease rates and operating expenses should be. Also, because you know of the mistakes I have made (see chapter 6), you won't overpay based on face rental rates that have no connection with reality.

Just 6 years later, in early 2019, this property was independently valued by Colliers International at $26.4 million, a 60 percent gain.

When you find a well-located, well-built property that has leases with multiple quality tenants renewing at different times, but don't have enough money saved up, what do you do? Do what most developers and entrepreneurs do: get help from friends and family. This is exactly what Jeff Bezos, now one of the richest men in the world, did when he first started out. According to a CNBC report, "In 1994, Jeff held 60 meetings with family members, friends and prospective investors to get them to each invest around $50,000 apiece in Amazon and help him raise $1 million. Only 20 said yes, a group which included his parents." In 1995, Jeff Bezos got his parents to invest $245,573 into Amazon.

So, if you don't have adequate funds on hand, ask a few family members and also start thinking about which of your friends you should reach out to. Because most people are looking for better returns than what their banks are offering, it won't take long for you to rustle up $200,000, $400,000 or more, perhaps even $1 million like Jeff Bezos did. Remember, you'll never get to second base if your foot remains on first. So, at some point, drum up the courage to take that first step to buy a property.

Built in just over a year during the Great Depression for about $40 million (plus $16 million for the building site at 34th Street and Fifth Avenue), the Empire State Building became a New York icon because of its record-setting height and its distinctive art deco design. In 1961, regarded real estate investor Harry Helmsley and partner Lawrence Wien arranged to acquire the Empire State Building from billionaire industrialist Henry Crown, who initially bought the building in 1951 for $10 million.

Helmsley and Wien purchased control of the Empire State Building for $39 million by securing a $6 million mortgage and raising $33 million from around 3,000 investors by selling them units of a limited partnership at $10,000 each. In the almost 60 years since the private placement sale of units to those 3,000 investors, the Empire State Building has paid about half a billion dollars in distributions to its limited partners and the building is now worth upwards of $2 billion. This is not to suggest that your investors will receive Empire State Building type returns, rather it's to suggest that real estate entrepreneurs have been relying on friends, family and other people's money for a long time. So, don't let the lack of capital hold you back from generating double-digit returns, in good markets and bad.

Once you have acquired the building you set your sights on, be sure to be communicative with your tenants and your investors, if any, regularly. Be honest and enthusiastic, treating your tenants like guests in a fine hotel, with respect and courtesy. Be sure to be disciplined in the upkeep and maintenance of your property, which should gleam with pride of ownership, easily setting your building apart from most other properties. Before you know it, your tenants (now your friends) will be referring others to you and also wanting to renew their leases, which generally speaking will be at higher rates.

In 2013, because I couldn't find acceptable returns in my own city, I expanded my geographical horizons and started looking at opportunities in Scottsdale, Arizona, one of the most beautiful cities in all of America, not to mention an easy 3-hour plane ride away. As recommended above, I met with different agents, lawyers, bankers and others to learn as much as I could about the market. Before I knew it, I was being presented with one opportunity after another. The first property I acquired was a 74,000-square-foot mixed-use office and retail complex, which was 92 percent occupied and sat on top of 10.6 acres of prime land close to the world-famous Mayo Clinic. This building is also near a major highway interchange and many other amenities, including the HonorHealth Scottsdale Shea hospital, which itself has 433 beds and a Level III neonatal intensive care unit.

This bank-owned property was up for auction and, with an in-place yield of 7 percent, I knew the complex would get plenty of interest from many savvy investors, which included a long-standing alumnus of the Forbes 400. While everyone was trying to get this beautiful property at a bargain basement price, I followed my rule of always being respectful and offered a fair price of $15.5 million (plus another $1 million in fees and commissions) and won the auction.

Remember, you are not getting a Rolls Royce for the price of a Mercedes, as discussed in chapter 4. I was so excited about being the highest bidder at the online auction that I took a screenshot of the winning bid on my iPad, which today is that much more memorable because I was in Paris during the time of the auction.

This is yet another example of why timing is more important than location, as discussed in chapter 3. Because

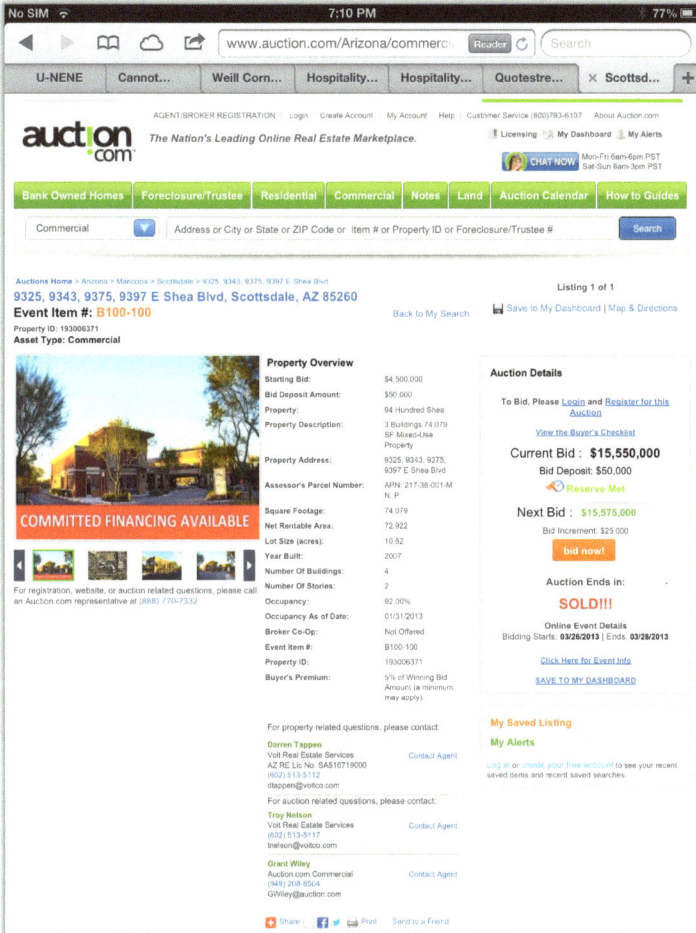

Screenshot of my winning bid taken on my iPad while visiting Paris.

the property was being auctioned, the winning bidder had to close within 30 days or forfeit a $1 million deposit. Since most banks don't move this fast, I had a write a check for the entire $16.5 million purchase price. Thank goodness I had this ability, as it offered me a competitive advantage over many others. Again, timing, timing, timing!

Although in great condition when my team and I acquired this Class-A 74,000-square-foot property, we went to work to make it even better. We began by resurfacing the parking lots, repainting the entire structure and added accent lighting on all buildings and most of the 20 or so trees. We also dramatically upgraded the landscaping to rival most any 5-Star resort hotel, which was tough to do because hotels in Scottsdale are among of the most beautiful I have ever seen.

Long story short, and by following everything I share in this book, the property was independently valued by Colliers International at $26.4 million on January 22, 2019. This $10 million increase in value works out to be a 60 percent gain in less than six years.

10 | MY NON-REAL ESTATE INVESTMENTS

Although riskier, I also invest in disruptive companies with significant upside potential.

Prior to the acquisition of my first commercial property back in 2006, I was primarily engaged in investing in public and private companies in which I would typically have a significant equity position. To this day, I continue to pursue such investments but on a substantially more selective basis.

Unlike my strategies and investment approach to buying real estate, when it comes to investing in technology companies, I prefer an "impact investment" style. My goal is to help smart inventors, entrepreneurs and scientists create and commercialize products and technologies that will have a beneficial impact on society at large. As a result, I have been a catalyst and financial backer of many small, early-stage companies over the years; some investments have been successful, some have not. In the end, most importantly, because good always begets good, if society benefits through my investments, even if my profit is marginal, I believe that society will always reciprocate.

By way of example, one of my first significant investments in the public marketplace was back in the mid-1990s. I invested in MedCare Technologies, a healthcare venture with, in my opinion at the time, lots of risk and lots of promise; it also had plenty of competition, including one company funded by George Soros (arguably the most prolific billionaire investor on the planet) that had $90 million in the bank (in 1996). In contrast, the company I invested in had just one full-time nurse on its payroll and a modest balance sheet.

While MedCare's major competitor eventually went bankrupt, the company I invested in flourished to become America's largest outsourced urology services company. MedCare eventually opened 100-plus medical clinics in one year, achieved a 90 percent success rate for the company's non-drug, non-surgical and non-invasive urinary incontinence treatment and rewarded its supporters with a stock moving from just pennies to the mid-teens per share on NASDAQ. Shareholders who held on were well rewarded for their investment. Unfortunately, following a change in management, the MedCare's fortunes were reversed.

I then acquired a controlling interest in a public company that was developing an artificial liver technology to help patients with failing livers live long enough to get a donor liver. Why would I make such an investment? Because my mother passed away from liver failure at just 57, an event that sent me into a deep depression for quite some time.

Having a functioning liver is vital. If your liver fails, you could die in a matter of days. According to Johns Hopkins Medicine, about 31,000 people die each year just in the U.S. from cirrhosis of the liver. More recently, the National Institutes of Health estimated that as many as 12 percent of U.S. adults have a form of fatty liver disease called nonalcoholic steatohepatitis, also known as NASH. So, when I had the opportunity to support a company developing a technology to help patients with failing livers, I jumped at the chance.

Named HepaLife, this company's most fascinating invention was a sort of "bionic liver" that did the job of a real liver. Bionic is somewhat of a misnomer because the proposed artificial liver was not meant for implantation in the patient's body. Instead, the equipment was to be external and the patient's blood would circulate through it. Just as dialysis performs the function of a patient's failing kidney, HepaLife's device was expected to perform the function of the patient's failing liver.

To accomplish this, HepaLife first had to find or create a "cell line," a line of liver cells that could live and divide virtually forever without dying or mutating. Swine cells were chosen because pig livers are biologically similar to human livers. The cell line that worked best was designated PICM-19, developed by two brilliant and gifted scientists at the United State Department of Agriculture, Drs. Neil Talbot and Thomas Caperna, both of whom I remain friends with and hold in the highest regard.

After a lot of effort to overcome early challenges, not to mention a good deal of my personal money, Drs. Talbot and Caperna and their team slowly started to make progress. As a result, the company's stock began to react favorably and increased in value. In fact, the PICM-19 liver cells performed so well that they were selected for testing by NASA.

HepaLife, the bioartificial organ company that I initially funded went onto acquire an advanced $60 million-plus Phase II/III bioartificial liver device. Unfortunately for society and the tens of millions who suffer from liver disease around the world, the Great Recession took its toll and the investor group I was involved with decided not to pursue further funding. This ultimately led me to sell the majority of my interest to a New York-based fund. The company, whose name was subsequently changed to Alliqua in 2010 by the New York investor group, is engaged in a different business now and its stock continues to trade on the NASDAQ stock market.

Now is a good time to note that if you are going to invest in public companies on the scale I have in the past, you must be prepared to face risks and obstacles that a typical investor would not encounter. This is best illustrated by the following example.

In August 2000, one of the companies that I founded and funded, EquityAlert.com, Inc. (a financial news and information redistributor) settled U.S. Securities and Exchange Commission (SEC) allegations that email disseminations made on a subscription basis by EquityAlert.com on behalf of various unrelated third-party advertising clients did not satisfy certain technical disclosure requirements. At the time, EquityAlert.com disclosed its compensation on a "dollars per thousand" emails sent basis, but the SEC wanted the company to disclose its compensation on a fixed total compensation basis. Without denying or admitting to the allegations, the company entered into a settlement agreement with the SEC, pursuant to which it and I agreed to pay $20,000 each.

In a second matter, EquityAlert.com accepted shares of an advertising company in lieu of cash. Even though EquityAlert.com had obtained an opinion of legal counsel stating that such shares could be sold without restriction, the SEC nevertheless alleged that the shares were transferred to EquityAlert.com by persons deemed affiliates of the third-party advertising company and hence were deemed restricted securities. And, because a registration statement was not filed for their resale, the subsequent sale of the shares by EquityAlert.com therefore allegedly constituted a violation of securities laws. In October 2003, not wanting to pursue a potentially expensive and lengthy defense of the SEC allegations, and against the good advice of my lawyer, to whom I should have listened, we agreed to pay $31,555 to settle, without admitting or denying, the SEC allegations. I was not personally required to make any payments.

Not wanting any more regulatory headaches of any kind, I voluntarily closed EquityAlert.com, despite it having 1 million subscribers to its real-time news redistribution service, which was significantly larger than TheStreet.com and The Wall Street Journal's combined online subscription base at the time. Ever since then, my team and I have been extra careful in all that we do, seeking and heeding

Electricity-generating windows from SolarWindow Technologies could turn entire buildings into vertical power generators.

the counsel of industry advisors, attorneys and accountants. As a result, we have not had a single regulatory issue in almost two decades while transacting many tens of millions of dollars in business.

Unfortunately, based on those two interactions with the SEC from almost two decades ago, some unsavory individuals, known as short sellers, have waged smear campaigns employing "short and distort" strategies over the years against me and some of the companies I have invested in. These short selling syndicates have intentionally tried to besmirch our highly regarded executives, scientists and industry thought leaders. Thinking nothing of the damage they are inflicting, these characters creatively present facts out of context to add credence to their hollow claims, all for the sake of making a quick buck.

In looking back, the valuable lesson I learned is that taking the most expeditious and cost-effective route in dealing with what you may think are simple technical infractions may not always be the best course of action in the long run. In retrospect, the reputational price paid was much higher than the relatively modest SEC settlement payments because the distorted information disseminated by the short sellers naturally was posted on the Internet, where it probably will remain forever, along with other anonymous postings and negative interpretations that pop up from time to time.

But no one is perfect. There have been plenty of hard-charging and ambitious entrepreneurs that have had their share of the spotlight. A while back, Richard Branson was convicted and actually briefly jailed for tax evasion. In 2010, Michael Dell paid a $4 million fine to the SEC. More recently, in 2018, Elon Musk agreed to pay $20 million to settle a federal lawsuit regarding a tweet about taking Tesla private. This is not to say that these amazing people are bad, it's meant to respectfully suggest that even the best of the best can and do slip up from time to time, as I did almost twenty years ago.

By now, you have no doubt surmised that much of what I do is a bit "out-of-the-box," not only in real estate but in other areas of endeavor as well. One of the most difficult truths of out-of-the-box thinking is that you open yourself up to criticism and potential failure. When you go against the grain of conventionality or invent a first-ever product like I have, you have to have the courage and personal conviction to keep moving forward, even with odds stacked against you.

Quite some time ago, while waiting for a meeting regarding photovoltaic nanoparticles at a major university, a crazy idea came to me from nowhere. In thinking about how small these photovoltaic nanoparticles were, it occurred to me that if they could be deposited onto a regular window, they would remain invisible while converting the incoming sunlight into electricity, essentially creating a transparent electricity-generating window.

Fast forward the clock by about 10 years, after shattering long-held engineering myths and overcoming many early disappointments, what started out as just a concept in the mind of a serial entrepreneur (me) may soon become a brand-new form of electrification. In my opinion as a stockholder and long-time supporter, this breakthrough could reshape the 21st century as dramatically and profoundly as the lightbulb transformed the last century.

According to the U.S. Department of Energy, energy from the sun is so plentiful that every week it produces 1,000 times the energy that oil, natural gas and coal does in a full year—combined. In fact, our energy needs can be easily met with just 1/10,000th of the estimated 173,000 terawatts of solar energy that strikes the Earth continuously.

Transparent electricity-generating windows have gone from just an idea to now a potentially industry-disrupting technology because of the dedication and hard work of John Conklin and the many scientists and engineers and supporting SolarWindow Technologies (www.solarwindow.com). SolarWindow is a public company that I founded and in which, to date, have invested approximately $30 million.

SolarWindow Technologies has set records, won awards and has even presented to members of Congress. The company has also been covered by numerous media outlets, including The Wall Street Journal, Engineering.com, Fast Company, Voice of America, Scientific American, National Geographic and CCTV, China's largest English language broadcaster.

SolarWindow is the developer of transparent electricity-generating coatings that transform ordinary glass into electricity-generating glass, which when fabricated into windows, could turn entire buildings into vertical power generators.

SolarWindow is initially targeting the estimated 5.6 million commercial buildings in the U.S. market, which alone consume almost $150 billion in electricity annually. According to independently-validated company power and financial modeling, SolarWindow's transparent electricity-generating windows could cut these energy costs by up to 50 percent.

The concept of electricity-generating windows is so exciting that whenever I meet with fellow building owners or real estate developers, you can literally see the wheels in their head start to turn. Their eyes light up and you can almost feel their hearts beat faster as they start talking about how to apply this technology to their existing and upcoming projects. Frankly, I can't imagine any commercial landlord, being one myself, not wanting electricity-generating windows.

And, perhaps more importantly, electricity-generating windows that could cut electricity costs by to 50 percent could be transformational, not only for building owners and the energy industry, but also for the environment and ergo for society in general.

Another public technology company I have supported over many years is RenovaCare (www.renovacareinc.com), which has developed the SkinGun™ to literally spray a liquid suspension of a person's own skin stem cells onto severe burns and wounds.

The SkinGun™ technology has been featured in many highly regarded publications, including Bloomberg, Forbes, National Geographic, CNN, Newsweek and O, The Oprah Magazine. Also, for almost a year, the SkinGun™ was on display at London's prestigious Science Museum.

In his best-selling book, *Money, Master the Game*, here's how Tony Robbins describes RenovaCare's SkinGun™ technology:

> "Every ten minutes in America someone is horribly burned. They're rushed to the hospital in searing pain—one of the most intense pains a human body can suffer. The nurses scrub away the blistered and charred flesh and cover the wound with cadaver skin to keep the person from dying of infection. Can you imagine the skin off a dead body put on top of your own?! If the patient survives, the scarring can be brutal. I'm sure you've seen faces, arms, and legs scarred beyond recognition. Sometimes there are multiple surgeries, and healing can take years.

Over 70 severe burn patients have been experimentally treated, with many leaving hospital in just days, avoiding painful skin graft surgery.

"So imagine how one night Matt Uram, a 40-year-old state trooper, finds himself about to become another one of those grim statistics. His life altered forever.

"How? He's next to a bonfire when someone throws a cup of gasoline on the flames, and the burns cover his right arm and the right side of his head and face. The doctors and nurses move fast, cleaning off the blistered skin, disinfecting Matt's wounds, applying salves. Normally he would be in the burn unit for weeks or months, going through the same agonizing process twice

93

a day. Instead, a team of specialists goes to work with a new technique. They harvest a layer of healthy cells from unburned patches of his own skin. No cadaver skin for Matt! These cells are cultured, and before long, a spray gun is gently painting the wounds with a solution of Matt's own stem cells.

"Three days later, his arms and face are completely healed. (And this miracle has to be seen to be believed! Go to youtu.be/eXO_ApjKPaI and see the difference.) There's barely a scar visible on him. I know it sounds like a scene from a sci-fi film. But it's a real story that took place in Pittsburgh just a few years ago."

Traditional treatment of burns and wounds involve surgically removing (grafting) large sheets of skin from the patient, which are then re-stitched onto the wound. This procedure has been characterized as painful, lengthy, expensive, prone to infections and scarring and, in many cases, requiring expensive pain and wound management.

In comparison, RenovaCare's SkinGin™ technology essentially involves harvesting a small postage stamp sized donor skin sample from the patient, from which the most regenerative stem cells are collected. These cells are then mixed into a water-based suspension and gently sprayed onto the patient's wound within 90 minutes of harvesting the small skin sample.

To date, the technology underlying the SkinGun™ has been experimentally used to treat over 70 severe burn victims, with many leaving the hospital in a matter of days while avoiding painful skin graft surgeries and potentially weeks of costly hospitalization. At this time, however, RenovaCare products are currently in development. They are not available for sale in the United States, and there is no assurance that the company's planned or filed submissions to the U.S. Food and Drug Administration (FDA), if any, will be accepted or cleared.

However, in my opinion, if RenovaCare is ever able to get any kind of FDA approval, it could be a boon to burn victims all over the world. This is why I have invested approximately $20 million since 2013.

As mentioned at the outset of this chapter, I want to help commercialize products and technologies that will have a beneficial impact on society at large. If society benefits through my support of companies like SolarWindow, RenovaCare and others, then, sooner or later, society will reciprocate in kind.

Remember: good always begets good.

DOUBLE-DIGIT RETURNS

ABOUT
HARMEL S. RAYAT

Harmel S. Rayat (www.harmelrayat.com) began as a clerk and messenger boy in the mailroom of a West Coast brokerage firm. Soon after, he became a stockbroker and eventually decided to invest full-time in 1987, just before Black Monday when stock markets around the world crashed. Early on, many of his investments did poorly; some even failed outright. With the help and support of many around him, he persevered through challenging times, both financial and personal. In due course, he learned how to deploy capital in much better ways and surrounded himself with an exceptional executive team.

He now manages a family office with a diversified portfolio ranging from commercial real estate to significant stakes in breakthrough technology companies. Although well-established, he has not forgotten about his early days as a messenger, delivering packages in the pouring rain to many downtown Vancouver buildings, including two that he proudly owns today.

CPSIA information can be obtained
at www.ICGtesting.com
Printed in the USA
LVHW071152120519
617519LV00044B/222/P